# Overcoming the Spirit
## of Grief

Word of Faith Publishing
Southfield, Michigan

Overcoming the Spirit of Grief
Copyright © 2002 by Keith A. Butler

**ISBN 1-931939-01-2**
**BK031**

Unless otherwise indicated, all Scripture quotations in this book are from the *King James Version* of the Holy Bible.

Published by Word of Faith Publishing
20000 W. Nine Mile Road
Southfield, MI  48075-5597

www.woficc.com
Printed in USA.

# *Table of Contents*

# Introduction

As humans, we are prone to accept grief, hold on to grief—even feed grief—and feel it is a natural process. However, the Word of God tells us that we should not accept grief, even in the most dire of circumstances.

When you do not deal with grief, you open yourself to further calamity. You open yourself to more grief. You open yourself to wounding the people you love. You open yourself to sickness.

In this timely, powerful message, Bishop Butler points you to Jesus the Anointed One who came to give you relief from grief! Regardless of what the enemy tries to do, there is one end result for a believer: Victory! Read on to discover the steps to supernatural restoration!

*Keith A. Butler*

## Chapter One
# *The Meaning of Grief*

Isaiah 53:1-4:

*Who hath believed our report? and to whom is the arm of the LORD revealed?*

*For he shall grow up before him as a tender plant, and as a root out of a dry ground: he hath no form nor comeliness; and when we shall see him, there is no beauty that we should desire him.*

*He is despised and rejected of men; a man of sorrows, and acquainted with grief: and we hid as it were our faces from him; he was despised, and we esteemed him not.*

*Surely he hath borne our griefs, and carried our sorrows: yet we did esteem him stricken, smitten of God, and afflicted.*

If you live long enough, you will experience times of grief. However, grief does not have to overcome you. Grief does not have to dominate you. Regardless of the situation, never forget what Jesus said in John 16:33:

*These things I have spoken unto you, that in me ye might have peace. In the world ye shall have tribulation: but be of good cheer; I have overcome the world.*

Thanks to Jesus, you can deal with the spirit of grief and keep it far from you.

The word *grief* in Scripture is translated from several Hebrew and Greek words with the following meanings:

- To suffer physical or mental adversity,

- To be vexed, angered, or in a state of indignation,

- To be wounded, weary, sick, or in pain, or

- To experience a malady, calamity, anxiety, or disease.

An individual overcome with grief may be vexed. He may explode in anger or lash out at others. He may become weak and weary. He may be open to affliction and sickness.

As humans, we are prone to accept grief, hold on to grief —even feed grief—and feel it is a natural process. However, the Word of God tells us that we should not accept grief, even in the most dire of circumstances.

*Keith A. Butler*

## *Chapter Two*
# *The Example of Job*

Look at Job, an individual whom we all would agree had reason to be overcome by grief. Job was the greatest of all the men in the East. He had a wonderful family. But he lost all of his wealth and possessions, and that brought him grief. He lost all of his children, and that brought him grief. In the midst of all of this, his wife turned against him. That, too, brought grief.

His grief was so great that his friends sat with him in silence for seven days and nights.

> *So they [Job's friends] sat down with him upon the ground seven days and seven nights, and none spake a word unto him: for they saw that his grief was very great.* Job 2:13

Job was vexed because of what Satan had brought to pass, and it made him angry.

> *Oh that my grief were throughly weighed, and my calamity laid in the balances together!*
>
> *For now it would be heavier than the sand of the sea: therefore my words are swallowed up.*
>
> *For the arrows of the Almighty are within me, the poison whereof drinketh up my spirit: the terrors of God do set themselves in array against me. Job 6:2-4*

As a minister for many years, I've counseled thousands of people who have been overcome with grief. When calamity happens, people often allow anger to overcome them. They lash out at God, and they lash out at the minister who is a representative of

God. They are bound by grief and need to be delivered.

Look at Psalm 6:5-7:

> *For in death there is no remembrance of thee: in the grave who shall give thee thanks?*

> *I am weary with my groaning; all the night make I my bed to swim; I water my couch with my tears.*

> *Mine eye is consumed because of grief; it waxeth old because of all mine enemies.*

When you don't deal with the spirit of grief, it becomes all-consuming. [The word *all consuming* means to make sick, to be weary and rubbed out.]. You can have great things happening to you, but grief will be the only thing that you can see. You can have victory coming your way, but if you hold on to the grief, it will consume you.

When you do not deal with grief, you open yourself to further calamity. You open yourself to more grief. You open yourself to wounding the people you love. You open yourself to sickness.

Satan loves it when you're overcome with grief. He wants to pile it on and keep kicking you until you are dead. **You cannot afford the spirit of grief! Grief will not change your situation, but it will change you—for the worse!**

## Chapter Three
# *Grief Because of Sin*

Grief can come to you for many reasons. In Psalm 31, grief came to David because of his sin.

> *For my life is spent with grief, and my years with sighing: my strength faileth because of mine iniquity, and my bones are consumed. Psalm 31:10*

Romans 6:23 says the *"wages of sin is death."* The word for *death* means death in all of its ramifications: physical death, spiritual death, financial death, emotional death, and relational death. God is against sin not because he is against fun but because sin opens the door to grief and death. Sin may feel like a high right now, but the end of sin is grief and death, and death will permeate all areas of your life.

Living holy before God is in your best interest. God wants you to live holy because He loves you. He knows that once you get out of His way and into the world's way, you are in a position where Satan can attack.

Look at Genesis 26:34-35:

> *And Esau was forty years old when he took to wife Judith the daughter of Beeri the Hittite, and Bashemath the daughter of Elon the Hittite:*
>
> *Which were a grief of mind unto Isaac and to Rebekah.*

When Esau married outside God's plan, his parents, Isaac and Rebecca, were embittered. They were grieved.

Today, families experience grief and bitterness  when children don't marry according to God's will. It is essential to teach your children God's plan for marriage as soon as they are old enough to understand. When my children were younger, I described to them what to look for in an ideal mate according to the Word of God. I explained to them from the Word of God why they were not to marry an unbeliever. I told them to make sure they married a true believer, not someone who just carried a Bible.

When my children became teenagers, they started talking about what they were looking for in a husband or a wife. By this time my words had made it into their hearts, and they had owned God's plan—it was now their idea, not just mine!

If you teach your children the truths of God's Word between the ages of zero and four, these truths will completely affect them. It is critical for you to invest time and share the Word of God with your child. If you don't, it will be too late to influence them when they are deciding who to marry.

Isaac and Rebecca were full of bitterness because Esau married somebody who didn't serve the God that they served. I'm sure Judith looked fine, but you need to teach your sons that a fine-looking woman who is not a Christian will lead him away from God and wind up destroying his life and drive a wedge between him and his family.

There is another side to this. Parents, don't stand in the way of your child's marriage if there is nothing wrong with the man or woman your child has chosen. If a young man who is interested in my daughter comes to me, meets the criteria and does the right thing, I am out of there. Now, if he isn't man enough to come and see me, he isn't a man! I am my child's covering of authority, and marriage is a transfer of that authority.

*Keith A. Butler*

## Chapter Four
# *Relief from Grief*

How do you get relief from grief? Look at Matthew 11:28-30:

> *Come unto me, all ye that labour and are heavy laden, and I will give you rest.*
>
> *Take my yoke upon you, and learn of me; for I am meek and lowly in heart: and ye shall find rest unto your souls.*
>
> *For my yoke is easy, and my burden is light.*

To find relief from grief, you go to the Word. You go to God in prayer. The words *heavy-laden* mean to be overburdened, and the word *labor* means to feel fatigue and wear. These are the very symptoms people have who are grieving.

The word *yoke* here does not refer to something around the neck of a beast of burden; it refers to a master teacher's instruction to a student. He says, *Take my teaching upon you and learn of me. What does My Word say about you losing your money? What does My Word say about somebody going to heaven early? What does My Word say about what is happening in your life?*

There is relief from grief! You go unto the Lord, and He gives you rest—ease, relief, and refreshment. In other words, the Word of God is healing balm to your scarred mind. It's healing balm to your broken heart. **Go to the Word of God first.** The Word is anointed, and the anointing of the Word will begin God's work in you.

When you experience a death in your family, you don't need a house full of people, even though that's our tradition for dealing with death. That tradition is not based on the Word. You need quiet. During this time, you need positive people surrounding you — those equipped to give you God's Word in the midst of the circumstance. You need someone who knows Jesus, to come and give you comfort. This is why you need to be a part of a church.

In the natural, some things are just too much for us. But, thank God, the supernatural is available to us. There is no area in this human walk that God has not already anticipated. There is no area in life for which God has not already provided a remedy. God never wants you destroyed. God wants you always to be victorious. But you have to be willing to cooperate with him.

*Keith A. Butler*

## Chapter Five
## *The Power of the Anointing*

Look at Isaiah 61:31-3:

> *The Spirit of the Lord GOD is upon me; because the LORD hath anointed me to preach good tidings unto the meek; he hath sent me to bind up the brokenhearted, to proclaim liberty to the captives, and the opening of the prison to them that are bound;*

> *To proclaim the acceptable year of the LORD, and the day of vengeance of our God; to comfort all that mourn;*

> *To appoint unto them that mourn in Zion, to give unto them beauty for ashes, the oil of joy for mourning, the garment of praise for the spirit of heaviness; that they might*

*be called trees of righteousness, the planting of the LORD, that he might be glorified.*

Isaiah is prophesying what the Messiah would say when he came to this earth. He would say *the Spirit of the Lord God is upon me; because the Lord hath anointed me.* The anointing is burden-removing, yoke-destroying power, as seen in Isaiah 10:27:

*And it shall come to pass in that day, that his burden shall be taken away from off thy shoulder, and his yoke from off thy neck, and the yoke shall be destroyed because of the anointing.*

Through the Messiah, God has made the anointing available for anyone who is willing to tap into it. The anointing removes anything that binds you. It removes anything that holds you down. How can you walk through something that was meant to hold you down? You can walk with the anointing! The anointing gives you strength.

The Hebrew word for *bind-up* means to wrap up firmly, to stop and to heal. The Hebrew word for *broken-hearted* means to burst, to break down, or to crush. In other words, He said, "I came to bind up those who feel like they are going to burst. I came to heal those who are broken down and lost. I came to heal those who are totally crushed. I came to make them whole."

God has many ways of making you whole, of restoring you. If you are about to burst, He will wrap His arms firmly around you. If you are broken down and crushed, He will wrap His arms firmly around you. He will restore you through His anointing.

There are people wandering the streets today whose lives and those of their families are destroyed because they never fought the spirit of grief. Marriages have been lost because one of the partners refused to overcome the spirit of grief through the anointing. When someone died, when some tragedy occurred, grief came in, and that person stopped being a partner and stopped being a loved one to his or her spouse.

You have to keep going even when grief has shattered your life. You still have a life to live. There is a remedy! Listen to Jesus reference Isaiah 61 when He reads from the scroll in Luke 4:17-20, proclaiming who He is and what He does now that He is on the earth:

*And there was delivered unto him the book of the prophet Esaias. And when he had opened the book, he found the place where it was written,*

*The Spirit of the Lord is upon me, because he hath anointed me to preach the gospel to the poor; he hath sent me to heal the broken-hearted, to preach deliverance to the captives, and recovering of sight to the blind, to set at liberty them that are bruised,*

*To preach the acceptable year of the Lord.*

*And he closed the book, and he gave it again to the minister, and sat down. And the eyes of all them that were in the synagogue were fastened on him.*

Jesus says that restoration is here because He is here. You may be in a bad situation, but He will make it better. You may feel like you are destroyed, but He will raise you out of ashes. It may look like there is no way you can go on, but if you will look to Him, He'll cause you not only to go on but also to strike a blow to the devil in the midst of the problem. But you have to stand against the spirit of grief. You cannot allow yourself to stay down.

## *Chapter Six*
# *The Power of Comfort*

Notice what Jesus said in Matthew 5:4:

> *Blessed are they that mourn: for they shall be comforted.*

Jesus the Anointed One came to comfort all that mourn. Mourning is a result of grief, but comfort brings consolation and ease. If you will receive and accept His anointing, you can have consolation and ease when you encounter tragedy. Jesus is called to give you that! He is called to give beauty instead of ashes to all those that mourn in Zion. He is called to give oil of joy instead of mourning, to give garments of praise instead of the spirit of heaviness. Why? That you may be called a tree of right standing with God, that He may be glorified.

The Messiah came even in the midst of sorrow to give you joy. The joy is your strength. Reach out to Jesus. Reach out to the Word. Reach out to the supernatural power of the anointing!

I liked going to the dentist when I was younger because he knocked me out with laughing gas before he performed any procedures! I don't know what he did to my teeth. All I know is that when I woke up, it was over. The gas enabled the dentist to do what needed to be done without me feeling any pain.

Now I don't recommend laughing gas; it can be quite addictive. But I am illustrating how the anointing works. The anointing is supernatural. You cannot feel pain when that anointing is flowing. I have known many believers who, in the midst of tragedy, have testified, "Bishop, I am just fine. I don't even know why I am fine." I'll tell you why they were fine. Jesus, through the anointing, was carrying them through that situation and they were able to function, and they were able to go on. They were even strong in the midst of it. You can't do this on your own. You must tap into His power and allow His power to be your laughing gas!

Let's review how this happens. When tragedy occurs, you go to Jesus and find out what the Word of God says on the subject or else you surround yourself with somebody who will help you find out what God's Word says. Then you make a decision to do what the Word says, even when you don't feel like it. God only wants you to take a half step forward, and He'll run the miles to you.

*Keith A. Butler*

## *Chapter Seven*
# *Say What God Said*

Notice the anointing in Isaiah 11:1-2:

> *And there shall come forth a rod out of the stem of Jesse, and a Branch shall grow out of his roots:*

> *And the spirit of the LORD shall rest upon him, the spirit of wisdom and understanding, the spirit of counsel and might, the spirit of knowledge and of the fear of the LORD;*

The anointing will give you the spirit of wisdom. The anointing will give you understanding. The anointing will give you the spirit of counsel and might. The anointing will give you the spirit of knowledge and of the fear of the Lord.

Are any human beings reading this? Guess what we human beings do? We make mistakes and leave doors open. We don't always grasp everything. The best among is us imperfect, and since we are imperfect, God has provided help for our imperfections. He has provided ways for us to operate, and one of them is through the spirit of counsel. When you go before God and pray in the Holy Ghost, things happen. When you get into the Word, things happen. When you tap into the anointing, things happen!

What did God tell Joshua when Moses didn't get to go into the Promised Land and Joshua had to assume leadership? Look at Joshua 1:8:

> *This book of the law shall not depart out of thy mouth; but thou shalt meditate therein day and night, that thou mayest observe to*

*do according to all that is written therein: for then thou shalt make thy way prosperous, and then thou shalt have good success.*

God told Joshua to say what God said: "Even if my lips are trembling, God loves me." Say what God said: "I am strong in the Lord and the power of His might." Say what God said: "God will restore unto me that which the enemy has taken from me." Amen!

When you start saying what God says, you tap into the tree of the anointing. The sap of the anointing begins to run down your arm. It begins to run down your entire body. It begins to run over your heart! When you make a decision not to be destroyed, Jesus and counsel will come to you. God will tell you what to do. When you go to prayer the

Holy Ghost will give you understanding.

God always has a ram in the bush. He is Jehovah Jireh. He is the one with provision, and He has provision for you if you tap into His anointing.

God is so good that even when we miss it, even when we leave a door open and the enemy attacks us, God makes a way out for us. The enemy may come in like a flood, but the Spirit of the Lord raises up the standard against Him. *Many are the afflictions of the righteous: but the Lord delivereth him out of them all*. Psalm 34:19

Paul said, "I may be afflicted, but I am not down. I am not going to be turned away by affliction. I am not going to be turned away by hunger. I am not going to be turned away by tragedy. What shall separate me from the love of God? Not one thing!

In all things I am more than a conqueror through Him that loved me." He is Jesus the Anointed One. Tap into His anointing.

*Keith A. Butler*

## Chapter Eight
## *Perfect Peace*

Read Isaiah 26:3:

> *Thou wilt keep him in perfect peace,*
> *whose mind is stayed on thee:*
> *because he trusteth in thee.*

When peace is perfect there is no open door for any of it to slip out. When perfect peace is manifested, there is nothing else that can get in. Why is his mind stayed on Him? Because he trusts Him. You may not understand why something has happened to you, and there are some things you will never find out until you get to heaven. So what do you have to do? Trust that He is good. Trust that He is merciful. Trust that He is fair even when you don't fully understand. Love Him, and you will find His power there for you.

Overcome the spirit of grief! Run it out. Grief is a spirit sent from hell to bring death to you. Don't give it any place. Some of you are still grieving over something that has happened in the past. Let it go! It is time to move on. You are going to make it! You are going to run that grief off, and when people see you they will be amazed because you have joy instead of grief. Walk through the valley of the shadow of death and come out on the other side. Even if you did mess up, His mercy shall follow you. Don't turn away from God; run to Him. Dwell in His house all the days of your life.

**Perfect Rejoicing**

Finally, look at Philippians 4:4-7:

*Rejoice in the Lord always: and again I say, Rejoice. Let your mod-*

*eration be known unto all men. The Lord is at hand. Be careful for nothing; but in every thing by prayer and supplication with thanksgiving let your requests be made known unto God. And the peace of God, which passeth all understanding, shall keep your hearts and minds through Christ Jesus.*

Scripture does not say, "Rejoice in the Lord only when everything is going well. Rejoice in the Lord as long as everybody is happy. Rejoice in the Lord as long as everything is working for you." No! It says to rejoice ALWAYS! It says to make your requests known unto God! And it promises that the peace of God will keep your hearts and minds through Christ Jesus!

When you rejoice always, you are not thanking God for what the devil did. You are thanking God for what He is doing. You are thanking Him that you will be restored. You are thanking Him that your heart will be healed.

You are not left without a way. You have a way, and His name is Jesus. He is the Lily of the Valley. He is the Bright and Morning Star! And supernaturally, He will give you the strength you need to overcome grief. Joy equals strength, so even if the tears are running down your face, find something for which to start thanking Him.

Now I am not telling you to do this legalistically. Don't misinterpret this message. When your friend is wounded, be gentle while you are helping him up with the Word of God. Then watch the anointing come in and take over. Your job will be done! The only thing left to do will be to shout victory with your friend!

Regardless of what the enemy tries to do, there is one end result for a believer: Victory! Praise Jesus!

If you have a wound in your heart, close your eyes before God and say, "In the Name of Jesus I stand against the spirit of grief. In Jesus' Name, I refuse to grieve any longer. Spirit of grief, I bind you and I command you to go from me. Father, I now ask you to let the anointing rest on me. Let the spirit of comfort and the spirit of counsel rest on me. In the Name of Jesus, I claim supernatural peace. I am made whole, I am healed in Jesus Name!" Hallelujah!

*Keith A. Butler*

## About the Author

Bishop Keith A. Butler is the founder and senior pastor of Word of Faith International Christian Center.

Word of Faith International Christian Center was founded on January 14, 1979, and is a congregation of 18,000 plus members and 250 employees. The main church is located on a beautiful 110-acre campus in Southfield, Michigan, where multiple services are held in the 5,000-seat auditorium. He is also founder of Faith Christian Centers in Smyrna, Georgia, which began in August 1993 and in Phoenix, Arizona, which began in September 1997. Until year 2000, Bishop Butler pastored all three churches every Sunday.

Bishop Butler is a pastor and Bible teacher with ministerial emphasis on teaching God's Word line-by-line and applying it to people's daily lives. He ministers in seminars, conventions and churches throughout the U.S. and in third-world nations.

Bishop Butler is also an author of more than a dozen books. He and his wife, Deborah, have three children who are all active in the work of the ministry: Pastor and Mrs. Keith A. Butler II, Minister MiChelle Butler and Minister Kristina Butler.

You may contact Bishop Butler by writing:

Word of Faith Publishing
20000 W. Nine Mile Road
Southfield, MI 48075
www.woficc.com

*Please include your prayer requests and comments when you write.*

## OTHER TITLES BY
## BISHOP KEITH A. BUTLER

Angels, God's Servants for You

A Seed Will Meet Any Need

Baptism

God's Plan for You

Hell: You Don't Want To Go There!

Home Improvement

How to Be Blessed By God

Making Room for Yourself

Receive Double For Your Trouble

Success Strategies From Heaven

The Grace of God: Faith to Receive
   God's Unlimited Promises

When the Righteous Are In Authority

▶ The Internet. It has the potential to communicate information and connect people in powerful ways.

Now it is bringing together Kenneth Hagin, Kenneth Copeland, Keith Butler, Jesse Duplantis, Creflo Dollar, Jerry Savelle, Mac Hammond, and many more for something historic... something with exciting possibilities for you, your family, and the world.

## THE TIME HAS COME

"Now you can join the online revolution, build your faith, protect your family and be a part of taking the Gospel to the world."

**CFAITH**.com
▶ YOUR INTERCONNECTED FAITH FAMILY

These well-respected ministries, along with many others, are uniting to connect the global faith family and reach out to others with the life-changing message of faith through the power of the Internet. They are coming together to launch **CFAITH.com**.